COLUMBUS CENTE
LIBRARY

VOLLEYBALL
everyone

Roberta Stokes

Miami-Dade Community College — South

and

Mick Haley

University of Texas

Hunter Textbooks Inc.

Consulting Editor: Dr. Clancy Moore, University of Florida

Copyright 1984 by Hunter Textbooks Incorporated

ISBN 0-88725-011-4

Printed in the United States of America

Cover Design and Illustrations by Deborah Dale © 1984 by Hunter Textbooks Inc.

All rights reserved. No part of this publication may be reproduced in any form whatsoever without written permission of the publisher.

Inquiries should be addressed to the publisher:

 Hunter Textbooks Inc.

823 Reynolda Road
Winston-Salem, North Carolina 27104

Preface

Volleyball is truly a game for everyone. It is well suited for participants of all ages, for boys and girls, for men and women, and for players of varying levels of skill. It can rightfully be categorized as a lifetime sport because extreme strength and stamina are not vital for participation. Volleyball lends itself perfectly to team play, leagues and tournaments for mixed doubles, and coed teams which are growing in popularity.

Volleyball Everyone provides the latest techniques to assist the beginning player in progressing to a more advanced level of skill. The unique format, which uses key words to explain the skills, should help players mentally visualize the correct technique for each skill. Numerous illustrations are included to aid the reader in understanding the various concepts. Other areas included are history of the game, terminology, serve receive patterns, offensive and defensive strategy, rules and special game situations.

Acknowledgments

The authors wish to express appreciation to the many colleagues, coaches, and players who contributed suggestions and insights.

Special thanks should be given to Jan and Bryce Corley and Carrie Haley from the University of Texas for the time devoted to posing for pictures and to Travis Spradling and Bob Zelinski for the photographs; to David DeGroote, who developed the very first key word camp manual concept; and to typists, Phyllis Seward and Carol Brown, who spent many hours on the manuscript.

The patience, encouragement, and guidance of Dr. Clancy Moore and Ernestine Godfrey are also deeply appreciated.

Contents

Origin and Early History

The game of volleyball was originated in 1895 by William C. Morgan in Holyoke, Massachusetts. He was serving as the physical director of the YMCA and wanted an activity that would be appropriate for large classes of businessmen — one that was not too strenuous.

Originally the game was played over a tennis net at a height approximately 6'6", and the object was to hit the ball back and forth over the net. Any number of players were allowed on a team. The game was first played with the bladder of a basketball but it was too slow and too light. Next a basketball was tried, but it proved to be too large and too heavy. Finally the A. G. Spaulding Company was asked to make a suitable ball which was similar to the ball currently used. The first rules allowed three outs before a team lost the ball and the game was played in nine innings. Actually the first rules incorporated many of the basic elements of tennis, baseball, and handball. Morgan called the game "mintonette."

Morgan presented the game at a YMCA Sports Conference at Springfield College in 1896. Dr. Alfred Halstead of Springfield College suggested changing the name to "volleyball" because of the way the game was played. The conference agreed to rename it and published a description of the game and its rules in the Journal of the YMCA. Since then the rules have gone through many changes as the YMCAs around the country made modifications to accommodate the special needs of those playing.

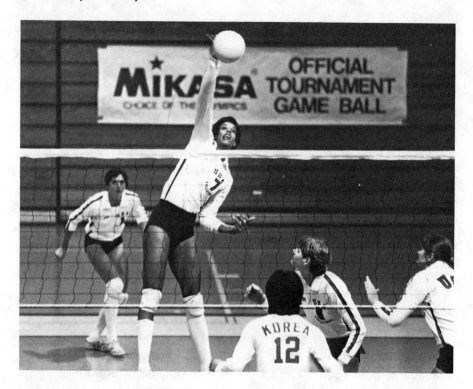

In 1928 the Volleyball Rules Committee of the YMCA was reorganized to become the United States Volleyball Association (USVBA). The group's purposes were to coordinate the volleyball rules on a national level and to create a national open tournament. The rules of the game, as well as information on various volleyball activities such as tournament standards and qualifying officials, have been published annually by the USVBA since its formation.

International Development

Volleyball was spread throughout the world by the International YMCA movement as well as by American troops during World Wars I and II who played the game recreationally. As the game spread, the style of playing and rules varied in each section and nation of the world. Attempts to organize an international federation during 1936 were unsuccessful, but in 1946 in Paris, such an organization was developed. France, the Soviet Union, Poland, Yugoslavia, and Czechoslovakia provided the primary leadership as fourteen other national federations joined them in forming the International Volleyball Federation

(IVBF). Other nations soon became affiliated and today there are more than 120 national federations in the IVBF.

The IVBF served as a catalyst for the increased popularity and growth of the game as it unified the rules and organized international tournaments. In 1949 in Prague, Czechoslovakia, the first world championships of volleyball were held. Ten nations competed in this championship, with the USSR winning. In that same year, the USVBA offered separate college and women's divisions at the national championships held in Los Angeles. At the Pan-American Games held in Mexico City in 1955, volleyball was included for the first time. The men's championship was won by the USA, and the women's by Mexico with the USA runner-up.

The inclusion of volleyball in the 1964 Olympic Games held in Tokyo was a significant event. The popularity of the game has increased greatly after the exposure of the 1964 Olympics, where the high level of performance and physical demands of the game were readily recognized. The men's division was won by the USSR and the women's winner was Japan.

Competition in the United States

The growth of volleyball within the schools, especially colleges and universities, has been a significant factor in its popularity throughout the United States. Currently all governing groups for collegiate sports conduct a volleyball championship. A brief history of these championships follows:

1969 — National Association of Intercollegiate Athletics (NAIA) held its first national championship at George Williams College in Chicago.

1970 — National Collegiate Athletic Association (NCAA) and the Division of Girls and Women's Sports (DGWS) held national championships. In 1971 the Association for Intercollegiate Athletics for Women (AIAW) was formed by the DGWS to conduct championship events for women. In 1982 the AIAW stopped operations when the NCAA began sponsoring championship events for women.

1973 — AIAW held the first Junior College/Community College Volleyball Championship at Miami-Dade Community College, South, in Miami, Florida.

1974 — National Junior College Athletic Association (NJCAA) held its first volleyball championship for men at Schoolcraft College in Michigan.

At the interscholastic level the popularity and level of play have increased tremendously. High school championships are being conducted by many conferences and states. Across the United States teachers and coaches are learning more about the game, and the influence of international competitions on the techniques and skills is apparent.

Opportunities for Playing

As the growth of volleyball has occurred, opportunities for playing the game, learning the skills and strategies, and becoming an official have increased. Numerous development camps for players of all ages are available throughout the United States. The USVBA conducts many such camps and officiating clinics in addition to sponsoring hundreds of

tournaments throughout the nation each year. The USVBA season generally begins in November and concludes at the National Championships in May or June. Tournaments are structured so that players at varying levels of skills are accommodated and encouraged to participate.

Many areas of the United States have encouraged year-round participation through the establishment of volleyball clubs. These groups are organized to promote and facilitate the playing of the game in that area. Although planned primarily for competitive purposes, they are also active at a recreational level. These clubs provide an opportunity for interested people outside of schools and universities to learn and enjoy the game.

Volleyball has become increasingly popular in recent years. The game of "power volleyball" challenges players not only to master the many individual skills of the game, but to develop the physical qualities of speed, strength, coordination, and endurance. Volleyball is an exciting, popular participant sport; and it is quickly becoming a popular spectator sport as well. Recent television coverage of the national college championship matches, Olympic play, and exhibition matches by our men's and women's national teams has contributed tremendously to the growing interest in this exciting sport.

Chapter 2

UNDERSTANDING
THE SPORT

THE GAME

Volleyball is a sport for everyone. It can be enjoyed by all ages. It can be played by those of varying skill levels: informally on the beach or in recreational leagues, or competitively at the interscholastic, intercollegiate or club level. The game can be played as the typical six-player game or in the doubles, three-player or four-player format.

Another feature which makes volleyball such a popular sport is that it requires a minimum of equipment — a ball, a net (with poles or standards) and an area at least 30 feet wide by 60 feet long will enable one to get started.

The basic objective of the game is to hit the ball over the net which separates the two opposing teams in such a way that the opponents cannot return it or that it hits the floor in their court. A team is allowed

three hits each time the ball crosses to their side, and the ball must be clearly hit in such a manner that it does not visibly rest on the hands or arms. Each rally begins with a serve and only the serving team scores points. A game is won when a team wins fifteen points with a two point advantage. An official match is usually the best of five games.

RULES OF THE GAME

The United States Volleyball Association is the official governing body for volleyball in the United States. The USVBA rules are those of the International Volleyball Federation (IVBF). These rules are used worldwide and have been adopted by all groups in the United States except the National Federation of State High School Associations. The NFSHSA has chosen to develop its own set of rules to govern high school play.

Individuals desiring to compete, coach or officiate should know the rules and league policies which apply to their situation. A basic outline of the USVBA rules is included to assist players in gaining a better understanding of the game. A complete set of rules is available from the following sources:

United States Volleyball Association
1750 East Boulder Street
Colorado Springs, CO 80909

National Federation of State High School Associations
P. O. Box 98
Elgin, IL 60120

National Association for Girls and Women in Sports
1900 Association Drive
Reston, VA 22091

The Court, Net, Ball

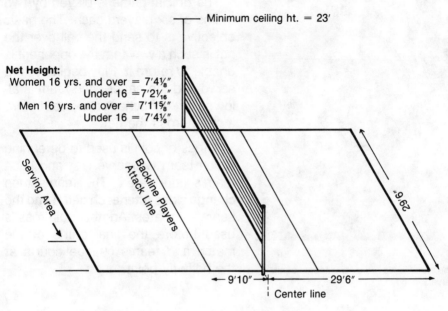

Minimum ceiling ht. = 23'

Net Height:
Women 16 yrs. and over = 7'4⅛"
Under 16 = 7'2⅟₁₆"
Men 16 yrs. and over = 7'11⅝"
Under 16 = 7'4⅛"

Serving Area

Backline Players
Attack Line

29'6"

←— 9'10" —→|←—————— 29'6" ——————→
Center line

The Official Ball

Laceless leather or
leatherlike cover

12 or more pieces of
uniform light color

5.5-6.5 lb./sq. inch
pressure
9-10 oz. in weight
25"-27" in circum-
ference

The game is played by two teams of six players each.

The Game

The official game is played by two teams of six players each. The basic objective is to send the ball over the net in such a way that the opponent is unable to return it. Play begins with a serve and thereafter each team is allowed three touches on the ball before it must cross the net.

A toss of coin is used to determine which team will serve first and each team's court area. The teams then change sides after each game and the serve alternates. Another coin toss is used before the final game of the match and teams change courts at the halfway point.

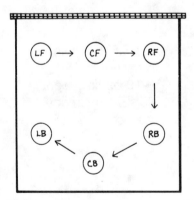

Players on the team scoring a side-out rotate clockwise one position.

Play begins with the service and if the serving team wins the play, a point is scored for that team. A side-out is scored if the receiving team wins the play. The players on the team scoring a side-out rotate clockwise one position and the player now in right back becomes the next server. A player must serve the ball within five seconds; the serve must not touch the net and the correct serving order must be followed. A game is completed when one team scores 15 points and is ahead by at least two points. A match consists of the best three out of five games, or in some situations (tournaments, tri-matches, etc.), the best two out of three games.

Players, Positions and Substitutions

1. At the start of each rally players must line up on the court with three in the front row and three in the back row. After the ball has been put in play, players may switch positions on the court. Back row players moving to the net may not attack or block. A back row player may attack if his or her take-off for the spike is clearly from behind the attack line.

2. Legal player positions require that a player cannot overlap with an adjacent player—the player directly in front or back and/or the players to either side. Overlapping is judged by the position of the feet at the time of service.

A team is allowed six substitutions per game.

3. A team is allowed six substitutions per game. Once a starting player is removed from the game, he or she can only return to the game once and must replace the previous substitute. *Note:* A currently used modification for the National Association for Girls and Women in Sport is that each player may enter the game three times and twelve team substitutions are allowed.

Ball Handling

All contact with the ball must be brief and instantaneous. When the ball comes to rest momentarily in the

Contact with the ball must be brief and instantaneous.

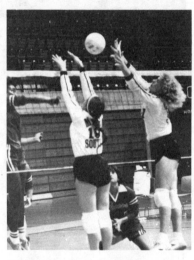

Players may not touch the net or cross the center line under the net while the ball is in play.

hands or arms of a player it is considered an illegal play (held ball). Scooping, lifting, pushing or carrying the ball are all considered to be forms of a held ball and therefore illegal. A player may hit the ball with any part of the body on or above the waist, but may only contact the ball once in succession.

Net Play

While the ball is in play, players may not touch the net or cross the center line under the net. Touching the court on the opponent's side of the center line is not a fault if some part of the foot remains on or above the center line. Players may not reach over the net and contact the ball before the opponent has completed an attack, but the ball may be played as soon as any part of it has crossed the vertical plane of the net. If a ball crossing the net is partially blocked, the blocking team has three more legal hits to return the ball. In this situation, the blocker is also allowed a second consecutive touch of the ball. When crossing the net, the ball must pass completely within the two antennas which are placed above the vertical tape markers at each end of the net.

Play Over

The following situations call for the serve to be repeated:

1. Two opponents contact the ball simultaneously above the net and the ball is momentarily held.

2. Two opponents commit fouls simultaneously.

3. An injury occurs during play and the official stops play.

4. A foreign object enters the court during play.

A play over occurs when the ball is momentarily held by two opponents.

Time Factor

Time Between Games: two minutes (5 minutes between the fourth and fifth games)

Team Time-outs: 30 seconds (each team is allowed two per game)

Substitution Time-out: The substitution must be completed immediately.

Player and Coach Conduct

Volleyball has strict rules in regard to player and coach conduct during a match. Violation of these rules of sportsmanship may result in a warning, penalty (point or side-out), expulsion from the game or disqualification from the match. The following acts are subject to penalty:

1. Persistently addressing officials concerning their decisions.

2. Making profane or vulgar remarks or acts to officials, opponents or spectators.

3. Committing acts tending to influence the decisions of officials.

Trying to influence decisions of officials may result in a penalty.

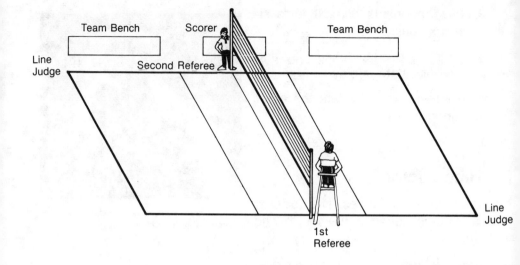

Team Bench   Scorer   Team Bench
Line
Judge   Second Referee
    Line
    Judge
1st
Referee

OFFICIALS

The officials for a volleyball match are a first referee, second referee, scorer, and two or four linesmen.

First Referee. This official is located at one end of the net in an elevated position that will allow a clear view of play. This person makes all decisions on ball handling plays, declares point or side-out, and has the power to overrule decisions of other officials. This official has full control of the match.

Second Referee. This official takes a position on the side of the court opposite the first referee. This person assists in calling violations regarding player position, the net, and the center line. In addition, the second referee keeps official time for time-outs and between games, supervises the conduct of coaches and substitutes on the bench, and supervises substitutions.

Scorer. The scorer is located on the side of the court opposite the first referee and behind the second referee. In addition to keeping an accurate record of the score and other pertinent information, the scorer notifies the second referee of any violations in regard to substitution, serving order, or time-outs.

Linesmen. The linesmen are positioned in the corners of the court in a position to see balls landing near their assigned boundary line. When only two linesmen are used, they stand diagonally opposite each other at the corners away from the serving area. By using a small flag, the linesmen indicate whether the ball landing near a line is "out" (raising the flag) or "in" (pointing the flag downward). In addition, the linesmen signal the first referee when the server commits a foot fault, the ball touches an antenna, the ball does not pass completely between the antennas as it crosses the net, or if a ball which is out was first contacted by a player.

Official Hand Signals

REMARKS:

1. All signals which are made with one hand shall be made with the hand on the side of the team which makes the error or makes any request.

2. After the signal is made, the referee points to the player who has committed the fault or to the team which has made a request.

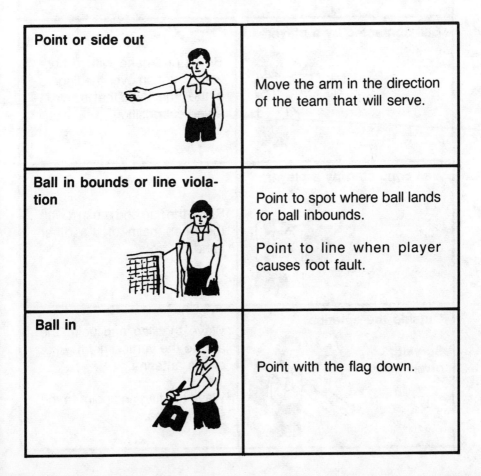

Point or side out	Move the arm in the direction of the team that will serve.
Ball in bounds or line violation	Point to spot where ball lands for ball inbounds. Point to line when player causes foot fault.
Ball in	Point with the flag down.

Ball out	
	Raise the forearms in a vertical position. Hands open, palms facing upward.
Ball out 	Raise the flag.
Ball contacted by a player 	Brush one hand with a horizontal motion over the fingers of the other hand that is held in a vertical position.
Ball contacted by a player 	Raise the flag and brush it with the open palm of the other hand.
Outside the antenna **Serving error** 	Wave the flag and point the arm to the vertical net marker or the antenna. Wave the flag and point to the serving area.

Four hits 	Raise four fingers.
Crossing center line 	Point to the center line and at the same time indicate with the "service" signal to the opponents' side; point to the player who committed the fault.
Held ball **Thrown ball** **Lifted ball** **Carried ball** 	Slowly lift one hand with the palm facing upward.
Double hit 	Lift two fingers in vertical position.
Ball contacted below the waist 	Point to the player who committed the fault with one hand and motion with the other hand from waist downward.

End of game or match	Cross the forearms in front of the chest.
Time out	Place the palm of one hand horizontally over the other hand, held in vertical position, forming the letter "T." Follow by pointing to the team requesting the time out.
Substitution	Make a circular motion of the hands around each other.
Ball not released at time of service	Lift the extended arm, the palm of the hand facing upward.
Delay of service	Raise five fingers in a vertical position.

Ball in the net at time of service **Player touching net** 	Touch the net with the hand. Touch the net with the hand and point to the player who committed the fault.
Double foul or play over 	Raise the thumbs of both hands.
Back line block or screen 	For screen, keep hands below top of head. For back line block, raise hands above top of head. Point to player(s) committing fault.
Out of position 	Make a circular motion with the hand and indicate the player or players who have committed the fault.
Over the net 	Pass the hand over the net and point to the player who committed the fault.

Back line spiker (attacker) 	Make a downward motion with the forearm and point to the player who committed the fault.
Ball touching object 	Point to the player or to the object touched by the ball.
Warning—Penalty—Exclusion	Show a yellow-colored card. Show a red-colored card. Show both the yellow and red cards. Call the captain of the offending team and advise the captain whether the exclusion is for one or more games or for the entire match.
Point 	Raise the index finger and arm on the side of the team that scores the point. **United States Only**

From the 1983 Official Volleyball Reference Guide of the United States Volleyball Association

GAME MODIFICATIONS

When the game is modified for special types of play, the rules are the same as previously stated except for the following.

Junior High School

The net height is 7 feet.

Coed Play

Men and women alternate positions on the court. If the ball is played by more than one player on a team, a woman must be one of them. Generally, the net is 8 feet high, and women specialize as setters and defensive players.

In coed play, men and women alternate positions and, when a ball is played by more than one player on a team, one of these players must be a woman.

Doubles

The court is shortened 5 feet on each end making it 30 feet wide by 50 feet long (30′ X 50′). A game is usually played to 11 points. Players stand side by side to receive serve, and the player not making the first pass moves forward to become the setter. Both players need to be able to set and spike.

Beach Play

Instead of lines to mark the playing area, ropes are used. Stepping across the center court below the net is legal unless you interfere with the other team. The serve may be made from anywhere behind the end line. The net height is 7′10″ on hard-packed sand and 7′9″ on loosely-packed sand. No antennas on the net are used, and the ball must pass within the wooden net posts. The ball used has a leather cover and is quite heavy in comparison to the official indoor ball. Teams change sides of the court every four points in an 11 point game or five points in a 15 point game. Players cannot reach over the net on a block, and spikers cannot follow through over the net.

ACE: A served ball which leads directly to a point being scored.

ATTACK: Returning the ball into the opponent's court by jumping into the air and hitting the ball from a height above the level of the net.

ATTACK BLOCK: A type of block in which the blocker attempts to contact the ball before it crosses the net.

BACKSET: A type of set in which the ball is set to a position behind the setter.

BALL HANDLING: The performance of any of the passing or setting fundamentals.

BLOCK: An attempt by one or more players to intercept the ball as it approaches or passes over the net.

COVER: (a) to defend an area of the court; (b) the positioning of players near a spiker or behind the block in order to retrieve balls which glance off another player.

CUTSHOT: An attack in which the ball is hit with slicing action at a sharp angle toward the sideline.

THE BACKSET

THE DINK

THE JUMP SET

DEFENSE: Strategy and tactics used by a team when the opponents control the action of the ball.

DIG: The technique used to pass the ball after an opponent's attack.

DINK (OR TIP): A soft, easy attack used to place the ball in an open area of the opponent's court; i.e., behind or to the side of the block.

DIVE: A technique used on defense to recover a ball by extending one's body in a prone position to the floor playing the ball with one or both forearms or fists.

FLOATER: A served ball that has little or no spin and follows an erratic path as it crosses the net.

FOREARM PASS: A method of passing the ball in which the ball is played off the forearms in an underhand manner.

FREE BALL: A ball which has been hit over the net with an upward flight allowing the opponent an easy play of the ball.

JUMP SET: A technique in which the setter jumps into the air to set the ball in order to save a misplaced pass or to confuse the block.

KILL SHOT: An attack which cannot be returned and directly results in a point or side-out for the attacking team.

LATERAL SET: A type of set in which the ball is set to either side of the setter rather than the usual forward or backward set.

MATCH: The winning of 3 out of 5 games (or 2 out of 3 games in certain situations; i.e., tournaments).

MIDDLE BLOCKER: The designation given to a specialist player who switches to the center forward position so as to block all plays at the net.

MULTIPLE OFFENSE: An offensive system designed with set plays using two or three hitters in a variety of attack patterns.

OFFENSE: Strategy and tactics used by the team controlling the ball which include serving, serve reception, setting and attacking the ball.

OFFSIDE BLOCKER: The front row player who is not participating in a two-player block.

OFFSPEED SPIKE: An attack made by hitting the ball with less than the usual spiking force so as to confuse the opponents.

OFF-HAND SIDE: The side of the court from which the spiker would have to contact the ball after it has crossed in front of the body.

ON-HAND SIDE: The side of the court from which the spiker would be able to contact the ball with the dominant hand before it has crossed in front of the body.

ONE-SET: An extremely low set, straight up above the net, which is quickly hit by the spiker as it leaves the setter's hands.

MIDDLE BLOCKER

ONE SET

OUT OF POSITION: An illegal play in which a player is not in the correct rotation order on the court at the time of the serve.

OVERHAND PASS: A method of passing the ball in which the fingertips of both hands are used to contact the ball in front of the face to pass the ball in the direction the player is facing.

OVERSET: A ball which has been set or passed that unintentionally goes over the net into the opponent's court and may be attacked by an opposing spiker.

PASS: The controlled movement of the ball between teammates.

PLAY SETS: Predetermined set variations used to create an effective attack situation. The ball is set with a variety of heights and positions along the net.

POWER VOLLEYBALL: That level of volleyball which requires greater organization and application of team strategy and individual skills than does recreational volleyball.

RALLY: Play of the ball between the service and the awarding of point or side-out.

REGULAR SET: A high, arching set that travels to the outside near the sideline.

ROLL: A technique used on defense to recover a ball by lunging and extending the body into a position to dig the ball, rolling over one shoulder and then returning quickly to a standing position.

ROTATION: The movement of players one position clockwise when a side-out is called on the opponent in order to prepare for the serve.

SCREEN: An illegal play in which one or more players on the serving team block the view of the server from the players of the opposing team.

SET: A pass made either overhand or underhand to place the ball in position for a teammate to spike.

SETTER: The designation given to a specialist player who has been select-ed as the primary person to set the ball to the spikers.

SHOOT SET: A medium low set which travels two to four feet above the net and comes down near the sideline.

SHOOT
SET

SIDE-OUT: The exchange of service to the receiving team when the serving team fails to score a point.

SOFT BLOCK: A type of block in which an attempt is made to deflect the ball for a teammate to recover.

SPIKE: An attack in which the ball is hit sharply and forcibly downward with one hand.

STRATEGY: The planned offensive and defensive techniques utilized by a team to take best advantage of the talents of individual players and thereby defeat the opponent.

STUFF BLOCK: An attack block which results in a point or side-out for the blocking team.

SWITCH: A planned interchange of positions on the court for offensive or defensive purposes. Movement of the players to another position must occur after the ball is contacted by the server.

STUFF BLOCK

TIP (OR DINK): A soft, easy attack used to place the ball in an open area of the opponent's court; i.e., behind or to the side of the block.

TOPSPIN: A technique in which overspin or forward spin is placed on the ball usually during a serve or spike.

TRANSITION: The adjustments in positioning a team makes as it changes from offense to defense or defense to offense.

"W" FORMATION: The alignment of players on the court for serve reception or free balls in which the five players form the pattern of a "W."

WIPE-OFF SHOT: An attack purposely hit off the blocker's hands, usually toward the out-of-bounds.

USOC: United States Olympic Committee

USVBA: United States Volleyball Association

WIPE-OFF

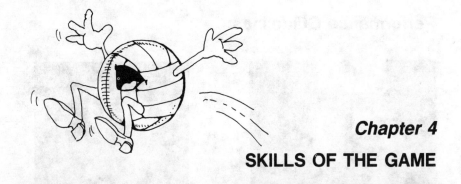

Chapter 4

SKILLS OF THE GAME

There are six basic skills to the game of volleyball: overhand pass, forearm pass, serve, attack, block, and spike reception. Each skill will be briefly described in relationship to its use in a game situation. Then a series of key words and pictures will be presented to guide the learner in executing the skill. You are encouraged to focus on the key words rather than trying to remember a list of performance techniques. By focusing on short descriptive words or phrases it will be easier to concentrate on those factors that ultimately determine successful execution of the skill.

OVERHAND PASS

Application: Used when passing a ball that is traveling very slowly and when setting the ball to the attacker. This method should be used whenever possible and is the most accurate method of playing the ball.

Performance Guidelines:

FEET SET

Weight on the back foot

Transfer to front foot on contact

Knees slightly flexed

Back straight

FACE WHERE YOU WANT TO SET

Hands raised above forehead

Shoulders, hips, and feet facing target

SHAPE THE BALL

Encircle the ball — form the shape of the ball with the hands

Contact with the pads of the first joint of each finger and thumbs

EXTEND TO THE TARGET

Maintain contact with an upward arm thrust

Hands and arms should follow the ball through full extension

Release the ball as quickly as possible

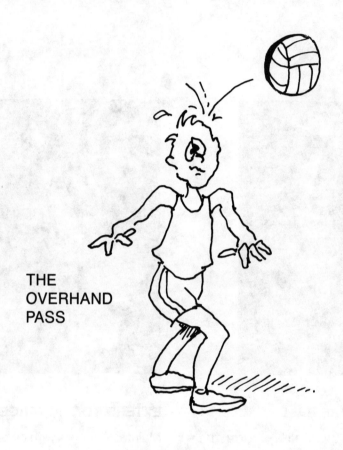

THE
OVERHAND
PASS

Common Performance Errors:

Lack of Control

Not maintaining contact with ball

Contact surface too small — encircle the ball

One hand ahead of the other

Incorrect or incomplete follow-through

Flexing the wrists rather than extending them

Not facing the target or turning to it too late

Not positioned directly behind the ball — playing it out to the side

Not playing the ball in front — letting it get on top of the head

Contacting the ball too low

Lack of Distance (Power)

Feet not set in correct position — front/back stride

Extending arms too soon — wait for ball to drop

Not using leg extension and pushing off from the floor

Inadequate Height

Not using leg extension

Lack of arm thrust upward

Bending too far forward

Illegal Contact

Jabbing ball with fingers

Fingers shift

Letting ball contact the palms

Trying to pass with the hands only — inadequate use of arm and leg extension

Ball Spinning

Lack of simultaneous contact by all fingers of both hands

Bending too far forward

Wrists twisting as ball released

One hand ahead of the other during follow-through

Not getting feet set

FOREARM PASS

Application: Used to receive serve, to pass free balls, and to control the ball in movement situations when the overhand technique cannot be used. This skill is considered the key to a team's success since all offensive maneuvers depend on the accuracy of the first pass. All players must learn to execute this skill well.

Performance Guidelines:

READY POSITION

Body perfectly balanced so that movement can be made quickly in any of four directions

PLATFORM TO TARGET

Arms straight and elbows locked

Hands together with hands contacting at thumbs first joint, the base of each thumb and the bottoms of both palms

Contact with forearms just above wrist

Contact in midline of the body

TRANSFER TO TARGET

Use only the arms to execute the pass

Weight shifts from back foot to front foot and into the ball

Common Performance Errors:

Ball Passed Too Low

Bending forward at the waist

Arms straight down in a vertical position

Ball Passed Too High

Too much leg action

Letting ball get too close to the body

Lack of Control

Contacting ball on the hands

Uneven contact surface — one arm above the other

Swinging at the ball

Contacting the ball to the side of the body

Platform not positioned to the target

Too much leg extension

Turning the body as ball contacted

Passing before getting feet set

SERVE

Application: Used to put the ball in play and therefore is the first offensive technique and the first way to score. It should place the opponents in a weak offensive position or score a direct point. The overhand serve is recommended except for the very young players; however, the serving team must place a majority of its serves in the opponent's court.

Performance Guidelines:

READY POSITION

Maintain good posture and keep muscles relaxed.

SQUARE TO THE TARGET

Face where you are to serve.

Common Performance Errors:

Lack of Control

Not square to the target — side to the net

Inaccurate ball toss — too far to the side, behind the player, too far forward, or too low

Arm not fully extended at contact

Contacting point on ball too high or too low

Not following through to the target

Flexing the wrist or "pulling" the ball down on the follow-through

Lack of Power

Inadequate backswing

No weight shift or body turn

Poor timing of movement into the ball

Incorrect contact surface of hand

Not maintaining a firm surface with wrist stiff at contact

Striking the ball too high or too low

Incorrect follow-through — across the body or not toward the target

PALM TO TARGET

Ball placed in the air approximately two feet above the tossing hand

LOOK DOWN ARM

Ball hit at center of gravity in direct line with flight

Wrist held stiff and arm at close to maximum extension

SPIKE RECEPTION

Application: Used to pass high velocity spikes, deflections, and some spinning serves by opponents. This exciting defensive skill requires anticipation (sometimes called an understanding of the opponent's tendencies, reading the opponent) and quickness.

Performance Guidelines:

READY LOW

Knees in front of toes, chin in front of knees, feet in a slight stagger position, weight on balls of feet, emphasizing forward motion.

STEP TO BALL — HIPS LOW

Step into the path of the flight of the ball, transferring one's weight forward.

As the body readies for contact with the ball on the arms, movement should be forward, moving from low to high or **up into** the ball. Never from high to low for contact.

ARMS GUIDE BALL

As the weight transfers into the ball, the platform should be tilted toward the target so that on contact the ball is propelled in the desired direction.

Depending upon the velocity, some follow-through is desirable.

Common Performance Errors:

Lack of Control (Ball going over net, off to the side, or too low)

Failing to get low to the ground — "under the ball"

Platform for ball not level

Swinging at the ball

Not moving in toward the ball

Too stiff on contact

Incorrect contact point

Poor Positioning

Reading "cues" incorrectly

Poor movement

Incorrect weight shift

THE ATTACK

Application: Used as the final maneuver in a team's offensive series to end the rally. Performing a successful spike to the floor of the opponent's court is one of the most exciting phases of the game. However, variations in types of attacks such as tips, dinks, wipe-offs, and changing the speed of the spikes and their placement can be equally effective methods of attack.

Performance Guidelines:

READY POSITION

10 to 12 feet from net

FEET TO THE BALL

Make sure the foot plant position for take-off is at the point where the player can strike the ball at the maximum height.

EXPLODE

Hips and shoulders are open.

Feet leave the floor quickly.

The arms are driven above the head vigorously.

As the arm is drawn back, the body travels upward toward the ball.

SWING UP OR REACH AND SNAP

The elbow of the hitting arm is rotated and leads toward the ball.

As the elbow snaps forward, contact with the ball is made in front of hitter.

Hand position is open and fingers slightly spread for control.

THE ATTACK

Common Performance Errors:

Poor Jumps and Lack of Height

Using one-foot takeoff, broad jumping into the net, approaching too soon

Failing to use arm lift

Approach either too fast or too slow

Lack of physical strength

Poor body angle on takeoff

Lack of Control

Using a closed fist

Failure to hyperextend and then flex the wrist

Hand is not "wrapped" around the ball

Lack of elbow rotation or snap

Hitting Ball Into Net

Jumping too late and contacting the ball too low

Too far from the ball

Failing to reach and fully extend the arm

Failing to rotate body square to the net

Hitting the Ball Long or Out of Bounds

Contact made under the ball

Approaching too soon and not contacting ball on back or top

Lack of elbow rotation or snap

Failing to keep ball in front — overrunning the ball

Poor Timing

Inconsistent sets

Trying to hit too hard

Incorrect approach angle and speed

Lack of sufficient practice

Lack of Power

Inadequate wrist snap or rotation

Failure to contract abdominal muscles

Incorrect contact point on ball

Poor arm action

Touching the Net

Approaching too fast

Broad jumping

Incorrect arm swing

Lack of wrist action

THE BLOCK

Application: Used to defend against hard-driven attacks by the opponent. This skill is essential to the defensive system when the opponent is capable of making a consistent and high velocity attack.

Performance Guidelines:

WATCH SETTER

Determine speed and height of set.

Anticipate where along the net the ball can be hit.

READ ATTACKER

Know attacker's position and what your hitter's tendencies are.

Concentrate on speed of approach, hitter approach angle, and distance ball has been set away from net.

READY POSITION

Hips parallel to net.

Hands high — fingers spread.

Slight flex of the knees.

PENETRATE QUICKLY

Place hands across the net immediately in the angle of the attack.

Once the hands do penetrate the net, the elbows lock, forming a barrier to deflect the ball.

There should be as little arm movement as possible.

THE BLOCK

Common Performance Errors:

Touching the Net

Jumping too far from net

Jumping forward

Swinging arms downward

Dropping head

Lack of Penetration

Weak jump — inadequate squat before jump

Poor timing — going up too soon

Not keeping hands high in ready position

"Missing" the Block

Incorrect evaluation of opponent's keys

Slow or late lateral movement

"Floating" in air after jump

Not placing hands in angle of attack

Fingers not spread

Hands too far apart

Ball Landing Between Blocker and Net

Lack of penetration

Late penetration

Not locking elbows on contact

PRACTICE DRILLS

The key to improving your skill is effective practice. The drills which follow are designed to provide a sequence for practicing each skill.

Overhand Pass

1. Assume the correct hand position on the ball — encircle the ball.

2. Place ball in hands and pass to floor — wrists and fingers relaxed.

3. Toss low to self and pass head high to partner; partner catches using overhand pass technique. Partner checks technique prior to tossing to self and passing to partner.

4. Sit and set drill: Have partners sit 8 to 12 feet apart and set ball back and forth. Emphasis on wrists and arms.

5. Partners 15 feet apart — set ball low back and forth. Keep hands and arms up.

6. Partners 10 feet apart — set ball high back and forth.

7. Set to self; set to partner.

8. Toss to self and pass ball high with same trajectory. Partner should allow ball to bounce in front and play it off bounce by passing high back to partner.

9. Set to partners left and then to right. Alternate and get foot patterns correct.

10. Set in front of partner; partner moves in, plays ball, and backs up 3 strides.

11. Set to self, set to partner, run around partner. Partner does the same.

12. Set to self, one-quarter turn, set to self, one-quarter turn, set overhead.

13. Triangle setting; reverse on whistle.

14. Set to self, touch floor with both hands, set to partner.

15. Set to self, make full pivot, set to partner.

16. Set triangle using two balls (3 players).

Forearm Pass

1. Passing action (arms only).

2. Passing a dropped ball.

3. Pass to partner off a bounced ball.

4. Pass to partner off a tossed ball.

5. Pass back and forth.

6. Pass ball tossed to either side (footwork).

7. Up and back movement — ball tossed by partner.

8. Passing tossed balls to target.

9. Pass, one-quarter turn, pass, one-quarter turn, and pass overhead.

10. Two tossers, one passer: Passer moves laterally passing balls back to the target from which they were tossed, working on foot patterning and arm swing.

Spike Reception

1. Throw at ankles — partner passes and checks body position.

2. Partner spikes ball from standing position — partner passes and spiker catches ball.

3. Pepper — one spiking, one passing. 20 then switch.

4. Wall drill — passer plays 10 feet away from wall. Thrower stands behind passer and throws ball against wall; passer attempts to react.

5. Have partner spike from floor to a target on the floor in front of partner. Partner will attempt to pass ball.

6. Instructor stands on table and hits ball to player to pass. Instructor tips ball periodically so that a dive and roll may also be used.

The Attack

1. Simulate arm action.
2. Spike a held ball to a partner.
3. Spike a tossed ball to the floor to a partner.
4. Four step approach — repeat 10 to 20 times daily.
5. Approach and hit a stationary ball being held by a partner on a table.
6. Spike a tossed ball.
7. Spike a set ball.
8. Spike a tossed ball 10 consecutive times, recovering each time.
9. Spike a tossed ball from left, center, and then right side of court.
10. Spike a set ball at targets on the court.
11. Repeat with two blockers.

Blocking

1. Jump and pike with shoulders, not hips.
2. Jump and penetrate net.
3. Jump and penetrate net, lock elbows, and throw ball to the floor with wrists only.
4. Partner on each side of net. One jumps and attempts to throw ball over and down, other partner penetrates for a block. Alternate.
5. At net, partner spikes ball into block.
6. Instructor on table spikes ball ahead, blocker practices attack block.
7. Instructor on table spikes against two blockers who attempt to area block.
8. Three tables, three blockers: Instructor calls a series of combinations. The hitters on the tables spike in staggered rhythm. Blockers attempt to react.

Serving

1. Throw basketball — alternate arms to 60 feet.

2. Serve from 20 feet. Work on form and technique.

3. Work up to serving 60 feet.

4. Work on serving accurately to areas 1, 6, and 5.

5. Change trajectories to areas 1, 6, and 5.

6. Serve to areas 2, 3, and 4 without changing technique.

7. Serve at whole team trying to find weaknesses.

8. Serving games:

    a. 3 point game

    b. Serving at passer in area. Count number of times out of 10 he/she can't pass ball to area.

    c. Target serving.

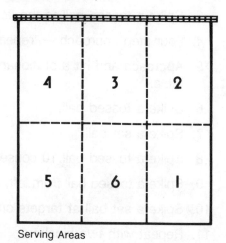

Serving Areas

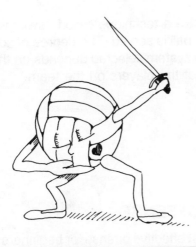

Chapter 5
OFFENSIVE SYSTEMS

The development of an effective offensive system will enable a team to utilize the individual strengths and weaknesses of its members most efficiently. The basic strategy of each system is to increase the occurrence of the pass, set, spike pattern of play.

Selection of a particular offensive system should be based on consideration of the following factors:

1. How consistently do players perform with precision the basic techniques — the pass, set, and spike?
2. What are the specific abilities and limitations of the setters and spikers? Can the setters spike and the spikers set?
3. What is the potential of all the players to learn an offensive system?
4. How much time is available to work on the complexities and coordination of the system?

Offensive systems are designated by the use of numerals: 4-2, 5-1, 6-2, etc. The first number in each system indicates the number of spikers and the second number, the setters. Once setters are determined, teams try to design a pattern which will isolate these players at the net during the serve so they will be free for the second play on the ball. Most players tend to develop greater proficiency in either setting or spiking and therefore teams utilize a technique called "switching" or changing positions just after the ball is served. The degree of sophistication of the particular offensive system selected depends on the individual talents and composition of the players on the team.

6-6 OFFENSE

Probably the simplest and most effective offense for beginners to use is a 6-6. In this system, each player has an opportunity to work as a setter and a hitter. There is no switching of positions so every player rotating to the center front position becomes the setter.

Although this offense is easily learned and helps a player attain the skills to be an all-around player, it has some definite drawbacks. Not all players will be equally effective as setters and hitters. In addition, if the team has one or more hitters who are extremely effective, offensive opportunities are more limited with this offense.

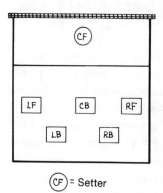

(CF) = Setter

4-2 OFFENSE

In this system, four players are designated as spikers and two players are selected to do the setting. Although occasionally spikers may be needed to set and setters may be called upon to attack, players are basically able to specialize in their strengths. The two setters begin the game directly opposite each other in the lineup. Therefore, one setter will be in the front row at all times, and the setter in the back row should attempt to set passes and digs deep in the court.

The front row setter always moves to the center of the court and close to the net as the ball is served. The attackers position themselves on the outside boundaries of the court. This gives them a larger area diagonally to hit the ball into (42 feet across court).

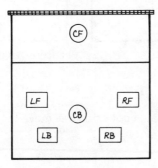 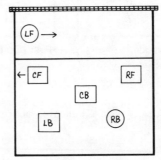

Since there is much less total team movement in this system, many errors are eliminated. Teams whose players possess only adequate movement fundamentals can still be efficient and consistent. Teams should probably stay with this type of offense until they have attained a high degree of proficiency in the basic skills and have players with the movement skills to handle a multiple offense.

The 4-2 System Lineup at Serve Reception

Since players may not overlap positions until the server contacts the ball, adjustments must be made in basic player positions to allow for the switching of the setter into position for the attack. The following diagrams illustrate the basic positions assumed by each player just prior to the serve and the movement of the setter.

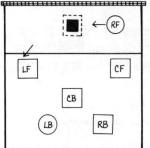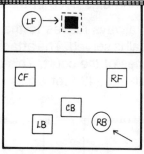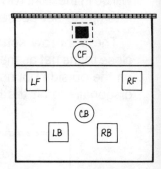

Starting Position   First Rotation   Second Rotation

Note: indicates approximate spot setter will move to.

In each of the first two diagrams, the front row setter moves to the center of the court as soon as the ball is contacted by the opposing server. In the third diagram, the setter's natural position is in the middle and therefore no switching is required.

The International 4-2 System at Serve Reception

A variation of the usual 4-2 offense involves the positioning of the front row setter to a spot approximately 6 to 10 feet from the right side boundary line close to the net. This allows both front row attackers to position themselves to the left of the setter, one in the middle of the court and one on the left boundary line. By having an attacker in the middle, more pressure is placed on the opposing center blocker. He or she must now guard against the center attack first, prior to moving to block the outside left attacker. This variation also eliminates the need for repeated blocking switches by the attackers and setter because the setter will be positioned in one designated area repeatedly.

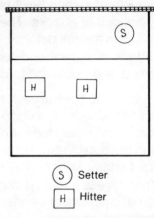

The following diagrams illustrate the basic positions assumed by each player and the setter after the serve.

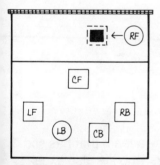
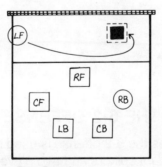
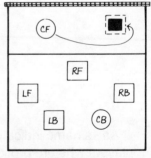

Starting Position   First Rotation   Second Rotation

Note: ▓ indicates the position on the court that the setter will move to in anticipation of the pass.

In each diagram the setter is positioned about 10 feet from the right side line immediately following contact by the opposing server. The attackers will then be spiking in only the left and center portions of the court at the net.

MULTIPLE OFFENSES: 6-2, 5-1

As teams progress in proficiency, they usually want to incorporate an offense which not only emphasizes player movement but allows greater variation in the attack—attacking from all three net positions, using a variety of setting heights and speeds, and varying the angles and net positions of attacks. The goal is to confuse the defensive team and/or result in a weak defense. The attacking team may be able to execute an attack at a spot undefended by a blocker, before the opponent can execute a block, and force the defense to commit to incorrect positions.

Basic to the success and strategy of the multiple offense is a quick middle attack. By forcing the opponent's middle blocker to concentrate on first stopping the middle attack, the blocker will have difficulty assisting the outside blocker on outside sets. However, teams that attempt a fast attack without the necessary skills may make many errors. Therefore, unless a team is certain it has the personnel with the skills and the time to perfect the system, most would do better to stay with the basic high set offenses.

THE 6-2 OFFENSE

As its name indicates the 6-2 offense is used by a team that has six players who are proficient spikers and two players who are also excellent setters. Since the setters are capable of attacking when they are on the front row, they assume a role of attacker and the setter on the back row penetrates to the net to set. Thus we now have a three-hitter attack — a multiple offense. Although players can position themselves to facilitate the quick movement of the setter to the net, it is important that the team have the ability to pass the ball accurately. The following diagrams illustrate the basic positions for a five-player and four-player serve reception using a 6-2 offense.

From a Basic 5-Player Serve Reception Formation

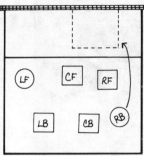
Starting Position

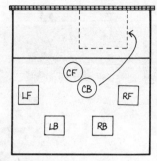
First Rotation

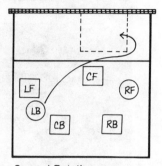
Second Rotation

In these positions, it is relatively easy for the back row setter to slip to the front row and into position prior to the ball passing over the net. In each case, the setter may not overlap prior to the serve being contacted. If the pass is good, this system will allow the team to have three spikers available to attack from three different areas. This will make blocking much more difficult for the other team.

In this rotation the setter in the left back position has a difficult move in front of the center front and center back, partially blocking their view as the serve is in the air. This move should be made quickly with the setter being in position prior to the ball being passed by a teammate.

From a Basic 4-Player Serve Reception Formation

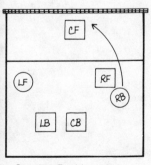
Starting Position

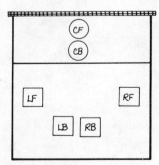
First Rotation

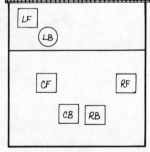
Second Rotation

The 6-2 Offense is used by teams with six proficient spikers of whom two are also excellent setters.

5-1 OFFENSE

The 5-1 system designates one player as the setter. The other five players then become attackers. This system actually combines both the 6-2 offense and the 4-2 offense. When the setter is in the back court, a 6-2 offensive system is run. When the setter has rotated to the front court, a 4-2 offensive system is run. An advantage of this system is the consistency of sets from a single setter. The following diagrams illustrate the positions assumed for a five-player serve reception and a four-player serve reception for a 5-1 offense.

From a Basic 4-Player Serve Reception Formation

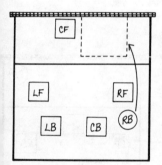

Starting Position

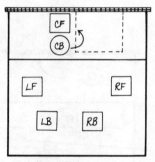

First Rotation

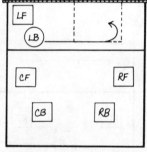

Second Rotation

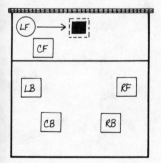

Third Rotation

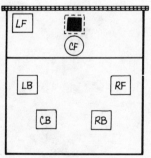

Fourth Rotation

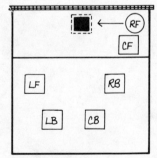

Fifth Rotation

From a Basic 5-Player Serve Reception Formation

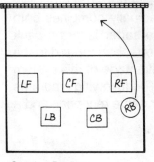

Starting Position

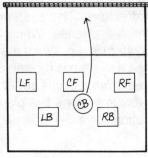

First Rotation

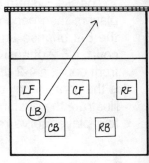

Second Rotation

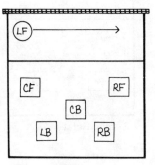

Third Rotation

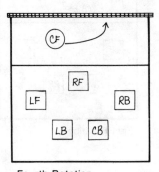

Fourth Rotation

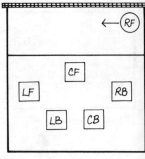

Fifth Rotation

Chapter 6

SERVICE RECEPTION

The key to establishing a team offense is accurate passing of the serve to the setter. Due to the current rule interpretations preventing the use of the overhand pass, the serve is almost always received with a forearm pass. The technique for correctly performing the forearm pass is described in Chapter 4.

Ready Position

While awaiting the serve, the player should assume a ready position with the knees slightly bent, arms relaxed in front of the body, and feet shoulder width apart with the right foot forward. Once the flight of the ball is known, the player should move quickly to a position behind the ball and stop before initiating the passing motion. The goal is to pass a ball with a medium high arc, no spin, and as little force as possible to the setter positioned either in the center forward position for a 4-2 offense or in an area between center forward and right forward for a 5-1 or 6-2 offense. As a team develops a more advanced offense relying on a fast attack, the use of a quick, low pass to the setter becomes important. A faster pass will allow the offense to form before the opposing blockers have an opportunity to recognize the attack patterns of the spikers and allow better timing of the fast middle attack.

"W" Formation

The most commonly used team pattern for receiving service is referred to as the "W" or 5-player formation—since there is a player positioned at each point of the "W":

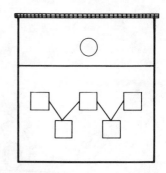

Basically, the "W" consists of a front line of three players and a back line of two players positioned in the spaces between the front players. The setter is the sixth player and is positioned close to the net, not to receive the serve but ready to receive the first pass. Although the "W" can be adjusted to be shallow or deep, usually the front line is in the middle of the court.

The "W" formation can be used effectively with either the 4-2 offense or an offense with three attackers. The only difference is that with a three-hitter attack the setter moves from the back row in order to be in position at the net when a teammate passes the serve.

"U" Formation

Another team pattern for receiving service which can be very effective is the "U," or four-player formation. Basically, the players assume the following positions:

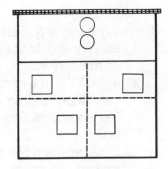

An advantage of this formation is that the middle hitter has more time to position for a quick set. In addition, the "U" formation enables the setter to position closer to the right front position before the serve. This formation also allows a team to "hide" a weak passer. It does, however, have several vulnerable serving spots — especially the short middle serve — and requires a team to be a strong passing team. It is possible to use this formation with any offensive system (4-2, 5-1, or 6-2).

General Guidelines

Regardless of the service reception formation utilized by a team, the following general guidelines should be observed.

1. Players should stagger themselves so that each has a clear view of the server.
2. In the "W," the center forward plays the first ball only if it is served very short and no one else can play it.
3. Serves above waist high should be played by the back row players.
4. Balls between two players should be played by the player moving toward the setter.
5. Front row players must "open out" and follow the ball as it goes behind them to be played by a back row player.
6. Players should concentrate on moving forward and laterally — not backward.
7. Good communication among players is essential. Players should automatically call "mine," "out," "short," or "deep" as a served ball approaches.

Chapter 7

DEFENSIVE SYSTEMS

Good individual defensive play and a well executed defensive alignment are essential to the success of any volleyball team. Without a strong defense, a team is limited in its opportunity to demonstrate its offensive skills. In addition, by developing an effective team blocking system, it is possible to score numerous points while actually "on defense." The defensive team is the team not actively playing the ball. A team is actually on defense when it is serving (even though the serve as an individual skill is an offensive technique) and whenever the ball is on the other side of the net.

It is extremely important for a team to establish its defensive ready position as soon as the ball crosses the net. All defensive systems are designed to establish an effective block, provide maximum coverage of the court by the players not blocking, and force the opponents away from their choice of offensive plays. Obviously, no one defensive system can accomplish this against all offensive systems. Not only are game situation adjustments in a particular defense necessary, but the ability to switch to a different defensive alignment may be beneficial.

Two basic defensive patterns are used today. Each has many variations or options and no one defensive system can guarantee success. These two systems are easily recognizable because one places a player from the back row approximately 10 feet behind the block **(player up defense)** while the other leaves the center of the court open by starting with four defensive diggers **(player back defense).**

For each defense, the exact starting position and final digging position of the players may vary according to the level of play, the spiking abilities of the various spiker, and a team's individual defensive abilities.

Good individual defensive play is essential to team success.

PLAYER BACK DEFENSE (2-4)

This system provides the strongest deep court defense against spikes. The name accurately describes the basic placement of players: 2 blockers at the net and 4 players positioned around the perimeter of the court.

Team Ready Position

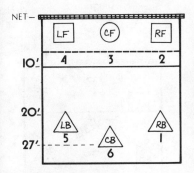 

Players 2, 3, 4: Positioned close to the net in position to form a double block.

Players 1 and 5: Positioned near the sideline and about 10 feet from the endline.

Player 6: Positioned on or near the endline.

Team Digging Position

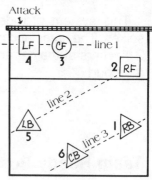

Diagram 1

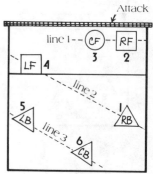

Diagram 2

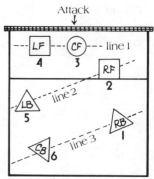

Diagram 3

In each defensive formation players have these specific assignments:

Blockers: First line of defense. Make certain block is together. Take away the power spike. Be aware of the ball and the spiker. The outside blocker sets the block at a position he or she believes the ball will cross the net. The middle blocker must move to take away the inside shot.

Offside Blockers: Drop away from the net and move in toward the block to recover deflections and inside dinks.

Diagram 1 = #2

Diagram 2 = #4

Diagram 3 = #2

Power Digger: Line up in the area where most hard spikes and power shots will be directed. Stay close to the sideline and be able to see spiker at all times.

Diagram 1 = #1

Diagram 2 = #5

Diagram 3 = #1 and #5

Player Back (#6 in all diagrams): Positioned deep in the court directly behind the center of the block. Covers deep hits and long deflections off the block but must be ready to dive for balls hit to the center of the court.

Player Behind the Block: Positioned near the sideline and responsible for ball hit down the line. Must also be alert for dinks or deflections off the block.

Diagram 1 = #5

Diagram 2 = #1

PLAYER UP DEFENSE (2-1-3)

This is a particularly effective defense when a team has strong blockers. It is used by many teams in a multiple offense; the back court setter is switched to the player up position to aid the transition to a setting position. The name of the defense once again describes the alignment: 2 blockers at the net, 1 player up behind the block, and 3 players positioned in deep defensive coverage.

Team Ready Position

 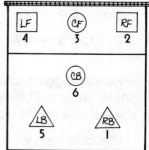

Players 2, 3, 4: Positioned close to the net in position to form a double block.

Players 1 and 5: Positioned inside the endline and approximately 10 feet from the sideline.

Player 6: Positioned behind the attack line and behind the CF player.

Team Digging Position

 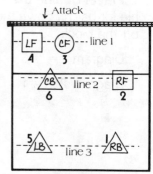

Diagram 1

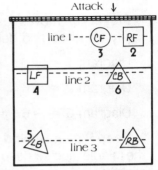

Diagram 2

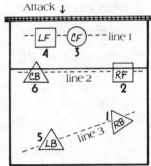

Diagram 3

In each defensive formation players have these specific assignments:

Blockers: First line of defense. Make certain block is together. Take away the power spike. Be aware of the ball and the spiker. The outside blocker sets the block at a position he or she believes the ball will cross the net. The middle blocker must move to take away the inside shot.

Offside Blocker: Drops back about 12 feet from the net near the sideline. Covers the inside power shot.

Diagram 1 = #2

Diagram 2 = #4

Diagram 3 = #2

Power Digger: Positioned to dig shots hit by the block toward the line.

Diagram 1 = #1

Diagram 2 = #5

Diagram 3 = #1

Player Up: Moves to a position behind the inside blocker. Stays low, ready for dinks and deflections behind or to the inside of the block.

Diagram 1 = #6

Diagram 2 = #6

Diagram 3 = #6

Deep Player Behind the Block: Positioned off the inside shoulder of the middle blocker deep in the court. Plays balls hit over, through, off, or slightly inside the block.

Diagram 1 = #5

Diagram 2 = #1

Diagram 3 = #5

CHOOSING A DEFENSIVE SYSTEM

A team must select the defensive system best suited for its needs. Since each defense has its strengths and weaknesses, adjustments during a game may be necessary to counteract the opponent's success. The following description of strengths and weaknesses for each system may assist with the selection of your team's basic defense.

Player Back Defense (2-4)

Strengths

1. Covers the "power alley" strong attack.
2. Covers the cross court diagonal hit.
3. Covers if there is a hole in the block.

Weaknesses

1. Off-speed and soft shots into the middle and just inside the block.
2. Down the line shots and deep hits to the corner behind the block.

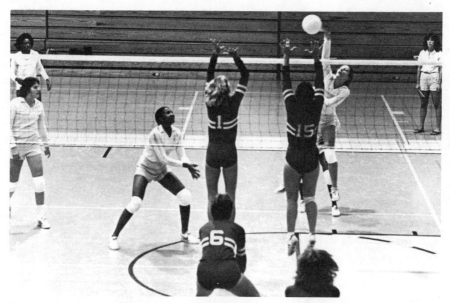

The strengths and weaknesses of a team should be the basis for selecting a defensive system.

Player Up Defense (2-1-3)

Strengths
1. Weak defensive players can be hidden by switching them to the player-up position.
2. The back row setter can more easily move to the net for offense when switched to the player-up position.
3. Soft shots over or around the block are well covered.

Weaknesses
1. Dinks and soft shots inside the block.
2. Coverage of the inside spike and balls hit directly over or through the block.

Obviously, correct positioning on the court is important to an effective defense. However, the ability of each player to "read" the spiker, to anticipate the play, and to execute the skill determines the ultimate success of a defense. The need for each individual to perform effectively within the defensive unit is vitally important. Much time and effort must be devoted to establishing any defensive system.

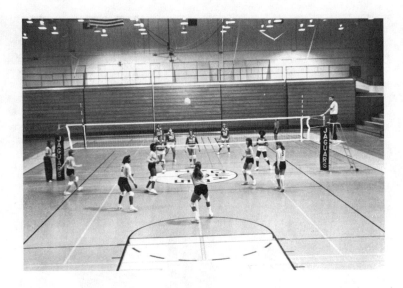

Free Ball Defense

There will be situations when the defensive team sees that the offense is not going to spike but intends to direct the ball over the net with an upward flight, weak spike, or forearm pass. At this time, the defensive team should call "free" and move into the position used for serve receive. Whenever possible this "free ball" should be played with an overhand pass. In a multiple offense, the setter must quickly move to the front row to receive the first pass. Experienced teams will attempt to use this opportunity to implement an offensive play.

The special situations described in this chapter are those requiring a player to use emergency measures to play the ball. Since the use of these techniques in a game situation is important, players should attempt to master these skills as soon as possible. Learning these techniques will not only save many points for the team, but aid in preventing such injuries as knee abrasions, hip and shoulder bruises, and split chins. By following a prescribed sequence for learning these techniques, players can avoid unnecessary injuries. In addition, when learning the dive and roll, players may wish to wear protective hip pads as well as knee pads.

Although these are advanced techniques, they are not beyond the reach of players who devote the time and effort to learning the correct fundamentals.

THE ROLL

Application: Used to recover from an attempt to play the ball in which the player quickly extends the body onto the floor to recover a ball which is just beyond reach.

Barrel or Lunge Roll
Performance Guidelines:

STEP TO BALL

Hips low.

EXTEND OR DRIVE THROUGH

Flex lead leg.

Extend other leg.

Shoulder Roll
Performance Guidelines:

STEP TO BALL

Hips low.

Weight forward.

EXTEND BOTH ARMS

Flex lead leg.

Extend other leg.

WHIP BOTTOM LEG OVER

Roll over lifting bottom leg.

STAND UP QUICKLY

Use arms to push up to ready position.

KNEE INSIDE, TUCK CHIN

Roll across opposite shoulder.

ROLL TIGHT TUCK

Kick both legs up and over the shoulder.

DIVE

Application: Used to play the ball by extending one's body to the floor in the prone position. It is especially useful in extending a player's range of coverage to retrieve balls that would otherwise be unplayable.

Performance Guidelines:

STEP TOWARD BALL
Keep body low.

DRIVE HIPS BELOW KNEE
Move arms forward.

CONTACT TWO ARMS
One leg kicked upward.

THRUST THROUGH WITH ARMS
Back is arched.

Head and chin up.

Absorb force with arms, chest, stomach, and thighs.

NET RECOVERY

A key technique needed to save a team from losing the rally is the ability to recover the ball after it goes into the net. If a teammate sends the ball into the net on the first or second contact by the team, it is legal to attempt to play it out of the net as long as no contact with the net is made. Once you have gained control of the underhand pass technique, the adjustment described below is relatively simple.

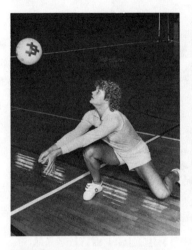  

Ready Position: Body sideways to the net, away from the ball's anticipated rebound.

Playing the Ball: The ball is played as low as possible to the floor to allow time for a good contact.

The Pass: The pass is made with a forearm technique directing the ball high to a teammate to attack (if it is the second contact) or deep to the other side (if it is the third contact).

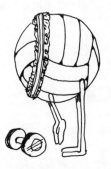

Chapter 9

READINESS
FOR THE GAME

Becoming a good volleyball player does not happen just by reading or devoting minimal time learning the skills of the game. Much hard work and practice must be directed to perfecting individual skills, to developing mental readiness to play the game, and to attaining top physical condition. The complete volleyball player is one who plays with knowledge, skill, physical stamina, and mental "toughness." Each player must determine the level of play he or she hopes to attain and realize that the ability to reach that goal depends on how much time and effort is devoted to achieving it. How well you ultimately play the game is directly related to how much effort and time you are willing to put forth.

Achieving a high level of play requires mental and physical readiness, the ability to force yourself to maintain total concentration and the discipline to push yourself physically. These are the qualities which separate the champion from the average player.

MENTAL READINESS

Mental readiness to play the game is as important as being physically ready. Total concentration on every play of every game of the match is what determines the really great volleyball player. As your role in the game changes you should think about the following:

When you are the server . . .

1. If your team is scoring points successively, serve promptly so as not to destroy the rhythm of the game.

2. If your team has just won a side-out, take your time serving to change the opponent's rhythm.

3. In the early and middle stages of the game, careful serves should be made.

4. In the final stage of the game, try to use a strong, powerful serve.

5. To avoid the opponent's quick attack, use cross court serves which cut off the communication between setter and spiker.

6. Observe the opponent's reception formation and use a serve that will move them up and back in the court.

7. Direct all serves to the one or two players who are poor passers.

When you are the receiver ...

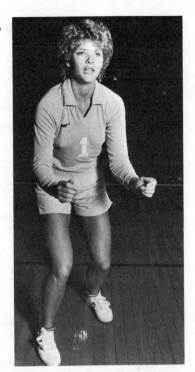

1. Concentrate on your position within the team's formation. Consider your distance from the net, position in relation to the end line and both side lines, and floor balance.

2. Assume the correct body position — a medium stance.

3. Maintain communication with your teammates.

4. Consider the particular server — the type, direction, and speed of the serve.

When you are "digging" a spike ...

1. Assume the lowest possible body position which will allow you to move freely.
2. Follow the ball. Determine who is going to spike by watching the set, and the direction of the hit by watching the spiker's body position.
3. Never give up trying to play the ball regardless of the power of the attack.

When you are the spiker . . .

1. Determine the players who will form the block against your attack.

2. Decide who is a good blocker, who is a high blocker and who is a lower blocker, and which blocker forms which side of the block.

3. Maintain communication with your setter. Let the setter know the type of set you want (but do not complain even if the set is bad). Deal with every set the best way you can — using various types of spikes, tips, overhand or underhand passes.

4. Always know the opponent's defensive formation. Is the center court area unguarded, are the deep corners open, etc.? Make your attack to these areas.

When you are a blocker . . .

1. Determine the opponent's spikers — point at them and say their numbers for reinforcement.

2. Decide your blocking position and the spiker you are responsible for covering.

3. If you have time, try to hop once or twice and then prepare to block. Concentrate on the position of your arms and hands.

4. On deep sets, the blocker opposite the spiker must decide and communicate to the team whether a block should be used. If no block is used, this blocker must drop straight back from the net.

5. Coordination between players in a block is critical: position close to each other, have similar timing, and call out when jumping.

6. In blocking a quick attack, the middle blocker must get ready for a quick jump by lifting the heels.

When you are the setter . . .

1. A reliable attack with accurate, safe sets is the offensive key.

2. The setter should control the pace and rhythm of the game. It is especially important to maintain the rhythm of your team — the same tempo as your daily practice. Know whether your team is best for a fast or slow rhythm.

3. Avoid all ball handling fouls such as holding or double contact.

4. Know which spiker is ready for the attack and set for him or her. If a player is not playing well, work with him or her, but go to other hitters to score.

5. Know your spikers and attempt to set the ball according to their special preferences.

6. Observe the opponent's blockers to identify weak areas and note their positions and movements. Use this to determine your attack strategy.

7. Utilize the planned offensive strategy according to the score of the game; i.e., outside attacks at the beginning, outside and quick attacks toward the end of the game.

When you are making a transition play . . .

1. Understand the importance of the switch from offense to defense and defense to offense.

2. When passing a free ball it is important to get the ball to the setter. If the setter is not yet in position, pass the ball high to give more time.

3. Whenever possible set the ball. Use care not to hurry your play.

4. When returning the last hit, make an effort to disrupt the opponent's play: return the ball deep to the corners of the court, return the ball high to enable your team to set up for defense, return the ball to the right side of the opponent's court to make a quick attack difficult.

When you are a substitute . . .

1. Understand the role you will be called upon to fill as a substitute. Are you a back row player? A specialist blocker? Attacker or server? A pacemaker to "fire up" the team?

2. Always be ready, mentally and physically, when your opportunity arrives.

3. Maintain a positive attitude and realize the importance of your role and the impact you can have on the outcome of the game.

4. Analyze your team's performance. Observe each phase—serving, reception and blocking position, offensive strategy—and be ready to communicate this to the players on the court.

5. Analyze your opponent's performance. Know the formations for spiking, blocking and reception in each rotation. Know what types of attacks are used and what type each spiker executes best. Know the best servers and what types of serves they use. Identify the weak passers and the type of formation used.

PHYSICAL READINESS

In order to become a top level player, it is essential to develop efficient movement patterns. Players must strive to gain good movement and body control. The ability to move with agility and quickness can be developed through attention to basic movement fundamentals and practice of these, just as one practices the ball handling skills of the game.

Basic Body Positions or Ready Positions

SERVE   **MIDDLE BLOCK**   **ATTACK**

High Ready Position:

Body erect and relaxed.

Used when serving, middle blocking, and attack approach.

SETTING

FOREARM PASS

Middle or Medium Ready Position:

1. Feet shoulder width apart — one foot slightly in front.

2. Weight on the inside part of the feet (not on the heels).

3. Knees slightly flexed with weight on the inside.

4. Weight is forward and back is straight.

5. Hands and arms are held away from body. Used when setting and for the forearm pass.

Low Ready Position:

1. Body is as low as possible but ready to move in all directions.

2. Anticipation of the attack angle and force are keys to good execution. Used for spike reception.

SPIKE RECEPTION

Movement To The Ball

Forward

1. Use normal running steps, or

2. Use a hopping motion — a step hop.

3. Prior to contact, both feet and hips should point to the target area.

Backward

1. Back peddling may be necessary after a player has moved forward to play a ball or cover a teammate.

2. Quick short steps should be used.

Lateral:

1. Use a side step or a step hop — step and then lift both feet off floor in a low hop.

2. Avoid cross-over steps.

3. Body finishes facing target area.

Movement Drills

Follow the Ball:

Instructor moves ball in various directions as players execute quick movements laterally left, laterally right, forward and backward.

Line Drills:

a. Using the lines on the court, have players run, touch a line and return to the endline. Movement in all directions can be included.

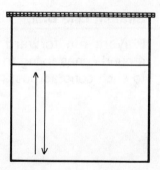

b. Using lateral movement (step hop), players move quickly between two lines (cones or chairs can be used) that are 8 to 10 feet apart.

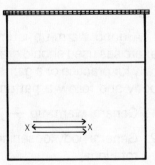

Box Drill:

Using the lines on the court, the players run forward to the center line (or attack line), move laterally to the opposite sideline, backward to the end line, and laterally to the starting point.

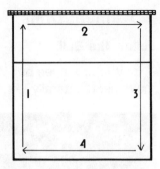

Slalom Drill:

Players move quickly by step hopping laterally around a series of cones placed in a staggered formation.

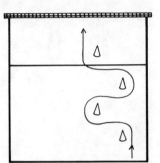

Straight Line Drill:

Players run forward or step hop around cones trying to stay as close to each cone as possible.

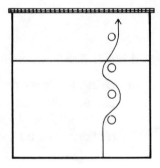

THE WARM-UP

A good warm-up is important at all levels of play. The drills and exercises used should gradually prepare the player physically and mentally for practice or a game. The warm-up should include all areas of the body and follow a pattern similar to the following:

1. General warm-up — jogging, movement and footwork drills.

2. General body loosening and limbering (arm circles, trunk twist, body rotations).

3. Stretching and flexibility exercises.

4. Vigorous exercises and coordination work (sprints, jumping, push-ups, rolls, dives).

Since the major sites of volleyball injuries are the ankle, knee, low back, and shoulder (neck), warm-ups should pay particular attention to these areas.

Another purpose of the warm-up is to elevate the heart rate gradually to approximately 120 beats per minute. It has been demonstrated that achieving such a heart rate during warm-up will not be too high to cause a drop in performance during competition; yet it will prepare the individual adequately by increasing body heat. It is important that individuals prepare sufficiently to prevent injury but not exercise so strenuously that a peak performance is prevented. The activities suggested above will accomplish this, but players should know how to check their progress. In addition to actually counting the pulse for 10 seconds (using the radial artery at the wrist), players will notice that a constant warm feeling with steady perspiration at the forehead, upper lip, palms, and under the arms generally indicates an adequate heart rate level.

Suggested Stretching Exercises

Stretching Exercises, continued

Chapter 10

EVALUATING SKILL
AND KNOWLEDGE

The following laboratory lessons are designed to help students and teachers evaluate the level of skill and knowledge of the game which has been attained. The skill evaluation involves players being rated on the key skills of the game. This will not only serve as a means of assessing players but give players a list of areas which need improvement.

The written questions can be assigned one unit at a time or as a final unit test.

Name_____   Date_____
                                  Rater_____

CHECKLIST FOR VOLLEYBALL TECHNIQUES

Following are a number of key checkpoints players should review to evaluate their progress in learning the individual skills. Have a partner observe you as you perform the following skills in drill or a game situation, and then rate you using the scale: 1 = Good, 2 = Fair, 3 = Poor.

General Movement

_____ "Extra" movements eliminated.

_____ Runs at a low center of gravity.

_____ Feet the minimum distance off the floor.

_____ Movement is made without bobbing.

Forearm Pass

_____ Right foot forward ready position.

_____ Right foot pointed toward the target area.

_____ Ball contacted at a level above the floor at about knee level.

_____ Ball played in an area between the hips.

_____ Pass initiated with weight shift from left to right in a direct line to the target.

_____ Hips rotate toward the target area.

_____ Arms finish no higher than parallel to the floor.

Overhand Pass and Setting

_____ Hands in extended position above forehead.

_____ Elbows only slightly bent and hands held forward.

_____ Momentum of ball moves hands back slightly.

_____ Arms and hands push ball out.

Serving

_____ Ball-held arm extended in the non-dominant hand.

_____ Dominant arm drawn back with open hand held high.

_____ Focus on the ball.

_____ Ball tossed approximately 3 feet above shoulder level.

_____ Hand strikes center of the ball.

_____ Hand and arm strike through the ball to the target area.

Blocking

_____ Ready position is approximately 10″ from the net.

_____ Hands held open at head level with arms close to the body.

_____ Feet shoulder width apart.

_____ Jump is from a deep squat.

_____ Hands in spread position with wrists extended and index fingers parallel.

_____ Outside blockers move in line with the extension of the hitter's attack arm.

_____ Middle blocker takes away the cross-court or the cut-back shot.

Attack

_____ Approach (for right handers): right, left, right, left pattern (last 2 steps occur almost simultaneously).

_____ Final step places foot almost parallel to net.

_____ Jump is initiated quickly.

_____ Hitting arm drawn back with hand held high.

_____ Abdominals contract causing body to pike as ball hit.

_____ Arm action is quick.

_____ Landing on both feet — contact with balls of feet followed by bending of legs.

Individual Defense

____ Ready position with weight forward, bent knee, head up.

____ Outside diggers with right foot forward.

____ Middle back has feet evenly spaced with weight distributed.

____ Body low enough to push arm platform between ball and the floor.

____ Push hips forward "through the ball" at contact with forward weight shift.

Rater's Comments:

VOLLEYBALL QUIZ

Name_____   Date_____

The Overhand Pass

1. Describe the ready position.

2. Where is contact of the ball made when correctly performing the overhand pass?

3. What usually causes the ball to follow a flat or downward trajectory instead of upward?

4. Why is it important to have the feet in a front back stride position when performing the overhand pass?

5. What determines whether the overhand pass is considered an illegal hit?

The Forearm Pass

1. Describe the position of the hands and arms.

2. What is the best position of the feet in performing the forearm pass?

3. List two uses of the forearm pass during a game.

4. Where should the ball be contacted?

The Attack

1. Describe the correct approach.

2. What type of *take-off* should be used?

3. What is a "dink"?

4. Describe the hand contact on the ball for a spike.

5. List two common errors in performing a spike.

The Block

1. Describe the ready position for blocking.

2. Describe the step pattern used by the middle blocker to move for a two player block.

3. Describe the correct hand position for the blocker.

4. List two common errors committed by blockers.

The Serve

1. Describe the ready position for the overhand serve.

2. Describe the contact made when performing a floater serve.

3. Why is the floater serve the most commonly used serve?

4. List two pointers mentioned in the book for good serving strategy.

Offensive Systems

1. Describe the 4-2 offense.

2. Diagram the position of all players in a 4-2 offense when the setter is in LF and the team is receiving serve.

3. Diagram the serve reception positions for a team playing a 5-1 offense when the setter is in CB.

4. Describe a 6-2 offense.

Defensive Systems

1. Diagram the base positions for the player—under the block defense and the center-back-deep defense.

2. What is the basic weakness of each defense?
   a. Player under the block?

   b. Player back?

3. What is a free ball?

4. State one factor that is important for defensive players to judge if they are to be able to anticipate the direction of the ball.

Name_____ Date_____

VOLLEYBALL RULES QUIZ

1. What part of the body is used to determine whether a player is overlapping?

2. What is the official's call if the ball hits an obstruction which is more than 23 feet above the court?

3. How many games must a team win in order to win an official match?

4. After the touch by a blocker, how many hits does that team have remaining?

5. May a blocker play the ball again after a touch on the block attempt?

6. Is it legal for a back line player to participate in a successful block?

7. What is the procedure when players on opposing sides commit a foul simultaneously?

8. How long does the server have before contacting the ball after the official's signal?

9. When may players exchange positions with another player on the court?

10. Who serves first in the second game of the match?

11. When do teams change courts in a match?

12. What type of ball is recommended for official indoor play?

13. How many times may a player legally enter the game?

14. Who serves first in the third game of the match?

15. Which parts of the body may legally be used to play the ball?

Write the CORRECT DECISION in the blank to the left of each statement. For all of the following, the RED team is serving, the BLUE team is receiving.

16. _____ A Blue player runs out of the court to play a ball that a teammate caused to go out.

17. _____ Blue player spiking and Red player blocking both hit the net simultaneously. The spike lands on the floor in Red's court.

18. _____ Blue team fails to return Red's service which had touched the net and landed in their court.

19. _____ Red player hits the ball into Blue's court, but steps on the center line in doing so. The ball is not returned.

20. _____ Blue center back rushes to the net and successfully blocks a spiked ball to the floor of Red's court.

REFERENCES

BOOKS

Bertucci, Bob (ed.). *Championship Volleyball by the Experts,* Leisure Press, West Point, New York, 1979.

Coleman, James, Consultant. *Power Volleyball.* The Athletic Institute, North Palm Beach, Florida, 1976.

Egstrom, Glen and Schaafsma, Frances. *Volleyball.* Wm. C. Brown Co. Pub., Dubuque, Iowa, 1972.

Furuichi, Suguru. *A Guide to Volleyball.*

International Volleyball Federation. *Coaches Manual.* Canadian Volleyball Association, Ontario, 1975.

Keller, Val. *Point, Game, and Match.* Creative Sports Books, Hollywood, California, 1968.

Keller, Val. *USVBA Level I Technical Module.* USVBA. Colorado Springs, Colorado, 1977.

Keller, Val. *USBVA Level II Technical Module.* USVBA. Colorado Springs, Colorado, 1970.

McGown, Carl, ed. *"It's Power Volleyball."* USBVA. Pacific Palisades, California, 1968.

Peck, Wilbur. *Volleyball.* Collier Books, London, 1970.

Peppler, Mary Jo. *Inside Volleyball for Women.* Henry Regnery Co., Chicago, 1977.

Prsala, Jan. *Fundamental Volleyball Contacts.* Canadian Volleyball Association, Ontario, 1976.

Sandefur, Randy. *Volleyball.* Goodyear Publishing Company, Santa Monica, California, 1970.

Scates, Allen. *Winning Volleyball.* Allyn and Bacon, Incorporated, Boston, 1976.

Schaafsma, Frances and Heck, Ann. *Volleyball for Coaches and Teachers.* Wm. C. Brown Pub., Dubuque, Iowa, 1971.

Schakel, David. *Volleyball — Fundamentals, Tactics, & Strategy.* American Press, Boston, 1981.

Schurman, Dewey. *Volleyball — A Guide to Skills & Strategy.* Atheneum, New York, 1974.

Shondell, Donald and McManama, Jerre. *Volleyball.* Prentice-Hall, Inc., Englewood Cliffs, New Jersey, 1971.

Slaymaker, Thomas and Brown, Virginia. *Power Volleyball.* W.B. Saunders Co., Philadelphia, 1976.

Thigpen, Janet. *Power Volleyball for Girls & Women.* Wm. C. Brown Co. Pub., Dubuque, Iowa, 1967.

PERIODICALS

Volleyball Review — Official Publication of USVBA. Published 4 times a year. USVBA Publication, P.O. Box 77065, San Francisco, California, 94107.

Volleyball Monthly — P.O. Box 4507, San Luis Obispo, California, 93403.

FILMS

Volleyball for Women — Featuring the U.S. Women's National Team. Introduction to basic skills, excerpts from international matches, slow motion and stop action. 20 minutes. 16 mm color and sound cassette. USVBA Films, 1750 E. Boulder Street, Colorado Springs, Colorado, 80909.

Power Volleyball — U.S. Pan American Games Men's & Women's Teams demonstrate techniques. Super 8 mm or standard 8 mm films. $19.95 each or set of 5 for $95. The Athletic Institute, 200 N. Castlewood Dr., North Palm Beach, Florida 33408.

Volleyball — Demonstration of the basic skills. Set of 6 films. Cost — $144 per set. BFA Educational Media, 2211 Michigan Ave., Santa Monica, California, 90404.

Volleyball — UCLA Coach Al Scates is author of these loop films produced by the Ealing Corp. Super 8 mm, silent, 3.5 minutes each, color. Cost — $24.95 each or $149.70 for a set of 6. NCAA Films, P.O. Box 2726, Wichita, Kansas, 67201.

COLUMBUS CENTER IUPUI
LIBRARY